This book belongs to:

_____

Contents

Cover illustration by Dave McTaggart
Illustrations on pages 32-33 by Peter Stevenson

Published by Ladybird Books Ltd
27 Wrights Lane London W8 5TZ
A Penguin Company
5 7 9 10 8 6

Printed in Italy

Magic spells

written by Catriona Macgregor
illustrated by Dave McTaggart

I'm just going to
turn you into a

I'm just going to
turn you into a

spider!

I'm just going to turn you into a

magician!

And **I'm** just going
to turn **you** into a

Don't bring that in here!

written by Marie Birkinshaw
illustrated by Sue King

Don't bring that muddy bag in here!

But why not?

Because it makes a mess.

Don't bring that muddy football in here!

But why not?

Because it makes a mess.

Don't bring that dog in here!

But why not?

Because…

we've made a cake!

Me too!

written by Lorraine Horsley

illustrated by Andrew Warrington

I'm going to play football.

I'm going to ride
my bike.

I'm going to read
a book.

I'm going to
watch TV.

Me too!

I've got chicken pox.

Where's the magician?

written by Marie Birkinshaw
illustrated by Russell Ayto

The magician's house,

the magician's well,

the magician's door,

the magician's bell,

the magician's book,

the magician's spell.

But where's the
magician?
Can you tell?

New words introduced in this book

bell

spell

tell

well

read

ride

because, bring, got, into,